Party Leaders in the United States Congress, 1789-2012

Valerie Heitshusen
Analyst on Congress and the Legislative Process

December 18, 2012

Congressional Research Service

7-5700

www.crs.gov

RL30567

CRS Report for Congress —————————————————————————

Prepared for Members and Committees of Congress

Summary

This report briefly describes current responsibilities and selection mechanisms for 15 House and Senate party leadership posts and provides tables with historical data, including service dates, party affiliation, and other information for each. Tables have been updated as of the report's issuance date to reflect leadership changes.

Although party divisions appeared almost from the First Congress, the formally structured party leadership organizations now taken for granted are a relatively modern development. Constitutionally specified leaders, namely the Speaker of the House and the President pro tempore of the Senate, can be identified since the first Congress. Other leadership posts, however, were not formally recognized until about the middle of the 19th century, and some are 20th century creations.

In the earliest Congresses, those House Members who took some role in leading their party were often designated by the President as his spokesperson in the chamber. By the early 1800s, an informal system developed when the Speaker began naming his lieutenant to chair one of the most influential House committees. Eventually, other members wielded significant influence via other committee posts (e.g., the post-1880 Committee on Rules). By the end of the 19th century, the formal position of floor leaders had been established in the House.

The Senate was slower than the House to develop formal party leadership positions, and there are similar problems in identifying individual early leaders. For instance, records of party conferences in the 19th century Senate are not available. Memoirs and other secondary sources reveal the identities of party conference or caucus chairs for some, but not all, Congresses after about 1850, but these posts carried very little authority. It was not uncommon for Senators to publicly declare that within the Senate parties, there was no single leader. Rather, through the turn of the 20th century, individuals who led the Senate achieved their position through recognized personal attributes, including persuasion and oratorical skills, rather than election or appointment to formal leadership posts. The formal positions for Senate party floor leaders eventually arose from the position of conference chair.

Owing to the aforementioned problems in identifying informal party leaders in earlier Congresses, the tables in this report identify each leadership position beginning with the year in which each is generally regarded to have been formally established. The report excludes some leadership posts in order to render the amount of data manageable. A bibliography cites useful references, especially in regard to sources for historical data, and an appendix explains the abbreviations used to denote political parties.

This report will be updated as changes in House and Senate party leadership positions occur.

Contents

Tables

Appendixes

Contacts

Introduction and Methodological Notes

Although party divisions sprang up almost from the First Congress, the formally structured party leadership organizations now taken for granted are a relatively modern development. Constitutionally specified leaders, namely the Speaker of the House and the President pro tempore of the Senate, can be identified since the first Congress. Other leadership posts, however, were not officially recognized until about the middle of the 19th century, and some are 20th century creations. The following tables identify 15 different party leadership posts beginning with the year when each is generally regarded to have been formally established.

The tables herein present data on service dates, party affiliation, and other information for the following House and Senate party leadership posts:

House Positions

1. Speakers of the House of Representatives, 1789-2012

2. House Republican Floor Leaders, 1899-2012

3. House Democratic Floor Leaders, 1899-2012

4. House Democratic Whips, 1901-2012

5. House Republican Whips, 1897-2012

6. House Republican Conference Chairs, 1863-2012

7. House Democratic Caucus Chairs, 1849-2012

Senate Positions

8. Presidents Pro Tempore of the Senate, 1789-2012

9. Deputy Presidents Pro Tempore of the Senate, 1977-2012

10. Permanent Acting President Pro Tempore of the Senate, 1964-2012

11. Senate Republican Floor Leaders, 1919-2012

12. Senate Democratic Floor Leaders and Conference Chairs, 1893-2012

13. Senate Republican Conference Chairs, 1893-2012

14. Senate Democratic Whips, 1913-2012

15. Senate Republican Whips, 1915-2012

This information reflects the leadership elections and appointments at the start of the 112th Congress, as well as changes that occurred during the Congress (as of the date of this report).

Included for each post are leaders' names, party and state affiliations, and dates and Congresses of service. For most Congresses, the report indicates years of service only, except in the tables for the House Speaker and the Senate President pro tempore, both of which include specific dates of service. When a Member died while holding a leadership office, however, the date of death is included as the end-of-service date (except in **Table 13**). In cases where a leadership change occurs during the course of a Congress, exact dates of service are indicated where possible. With respect to length of service, the report includes all instances in which a Member held a particular leadership post, regardless of whether the Member held the post for the entire Congress or only a portion of it.

Official congressional documents (*House Journal* and *Senate Journal*, *Congressional Record*, and predecessor publications) can be used to document the tenure of the constitutionally specified leaders (i.e., Speaker and President pro tempore). The actions of the party organizations in choosing other leaders, such as floor leaders or caucus or conference chairs, frequently went unacknowledged in these sources, however. In the frequent absence of party caucus records in the latter half of the 19th century, scholars have had to rely on secondary sources, such as memoirs and correspondence, for evidence of party leadership position-holding. The concluding portion of this report, "Source Notes and Bibliography," provides more information about sources and the reliability of leadership lists.

Identifying House Leaders

The changing nature of congressional leadership provides additional challenges to identifying leaders not constitutionally specified (e.g., floor leader).[1] Even for party elected posts, determining who held other positions can be problematic in earlier Congresses. For example, identifying each party's conference (or caucus) chair often requires reliance on incomplete historical records of conference meetings or inferences made from informal practices (e.g., noting which Member nominated his party's candidate for Speaker, a motion that often fell to the conference chair).

In the House, for example, it was the common practice of President Thomas Jefferson and his immediate successors to designate a Member as their principal legislative spokesman. Often these spokesmen held no other formal leadership position in the House, and Presidents frequently designated new spokesmen, or even specialized spokesmen for individual measures, as their terms progressed. As these and other "leaders" were not chosen by a congressional party group or by a party leader such as the Speaker, these presidential designees have not been included here as "party leaders."

Most historians who study the 19th century House acknowledge that an informal "positional leadership" system emerged possibly as early as the "War Hawk" Congress (1811-1813) under Speaker Henry Clay. Under this system, the Speaker—who at the time designated the chairmen of the standing committees—would name his principal lieutenant to be chairman of the Ways and Means Committee. After the Appropriations Committee was split from the Ways and Means Committee in 1865, the Speaker's principal floor lieutenant received either of these chairs. Sometimes, the Speaker chose a rival for the speakership to chair one of these committees in an effort to resolve intra-party disputes.

---

[1] See the "Source Notes and Bibliography" section at the end of this report for a description and citation of the multiple sources used in identifying leaders in the House of Representatives.

It is somewhat inaccurate, however, to consider these early leaders to be majority leaders in the modern sense, and they have not been included here. The position of chair of the Appropriations or Ways and Means Committee inevitably made the incumbent a powerful congressional figure because of the important legislation reported from these committees. These chairs were not, however, chosen in a vote by the full party organization, as the majority or minority House leaders are now. Furthermore, other leading congressional figures, such as the Republican leader Thomas Brackett Reed, achieved their positions of influence within the House by service on other committees, such as—in Reed's case—the post-1880 Rules Committee.

Identifying Senate Leaders

The Senate developed an identifiable party leadership later than the House. The few existing records of party conferences in the 19th century Senate are held in private collections. Memoirs and other secondary sources reveal the identities of party conference or caucus chairs for some, but not all, Congresses after about 1850; these posts, however, carried very little authority. It was not uncommon for Senators to declare publicly that within the Senate parties there was no single leader.[2] Instead, through the turn of the 20th century, individuals who led the Senate achieved their position through recognized personal attributes, including persuasion and oratory skills, rather than the current practice of election to most official leadership posts.

The development of Senate party floor leaders was one of slow evolution, like the House, but they arose for the most part from the post of conference chair. Not until 1945 did Senate Republicans specify that the conference chair and floor leader posts must be held by separate Senators. Among Senate Democrats, the floor leader is also chair of the conference. In many secondary sources, Senators are identified as "floor leaders" before existing party conference records so identify them. In this report, footnotes to the tables attempt to clarify when a leader was identified through official sources such as caucus minutes or through secondary sources.

Party Affiliation Designations

Another problem in identifying party leaders in early Congresses is the matter of party affiliation. Secondary sources reporting on party leaders often relied upon the information compiled in early editions of the *Biographical Directory of the United States Congress*. As the editors of the 1989 edition of the *Biographical Directory* noted:

> The most serious source of error and confusion in previous editions [of the *Biographical Directory*] [was] the designations of party affiliation. Many of the party labels added to the editions of 1913 and 1928 were anachronistic, claiming for the two modern parties Senators and Representatives elected to Congress before the [modern] Democratic or Republican parties existed. Other entries ignored the frequent shifts in party affiliation during the nineteenth century or omitted reference to short-lived and regional political parties and thus failed to reflect the vigor and diversity of nineteenth-century politics.[3]

---

[2] Woodrow Wilson, *Congressional Government* (Boston: Houghton-Mifflin, 1885), p. 223.

[3] U.S. Congress, Senate, *Biographical Directory of the United States Congress 1774-1989: the Continental Congress, September 5, 1774, to October 21, 1788*, and *The Congress of the United States, from the First through the One Hundredth Congresses, March 4, 1789, to January 3, 1989, inclusive*, Bicentennial edition, S.Doc. 100-34, 100th Cong., 2nd sess. (Washington: GPO, 1989), p. 3.

The 1989 and 1997 editions of the *Biographical Directory* resolved these differences, and their designations of party affiliations are principal sources for this report. The 1997 edition of the *Biographical Directory,* in particular, included more complete notations where Members changed their party affiliations while serving in Congress.[4] The main source for early party affiliations of Senator leaders, principally Presidents pro tempore, is volume four of Senator Robert C. Byrd's *The Senate, 1789-1989. (Historical Statistics, 1789-1992).*[5] An **Appendix** explains the abbreviations used to denote party affiliations in this report.

Leadership Posts Excluded

The tables in this report exclude some leadership posts in order to render manageable the amount of data provided. Specifically, the Senate and House party conference secretaries, and the chairs of party committees (e.g., steering committees, policy committees, committees on committees, and campaign committees) are not presented here. Junior party whips are also not identified. At least since the 1930s in the House, both parties have selected (or allowed the principal whip to designate) subordinate whips. The lack of adequate records makes it almost impossible to identify all deputy whips, regional whips, and zone whips who have been appointed in the last 70 years.

House Positions: Descriptions and Historical Tables

Speaker of the House of Representatives

The position of Speaker is constitutionally specified in Article 1, Section 2. The Speaker is the only party leader who is chosen by a roll-call vote of the full House of Representatives, which occurs after each party has nominated a candidate for the position when a new Congress convenes. House rules give the Speaker various formal duties. These include, for example, administering the oath of office to new Members, signing House-passed bills and resolutions, presiding over the House (and making rulings on the presence of a quorum, points of order, etc.), referring measures to committees, and naming the party's slate of members for certain committee positions. Each party conference cedes additional powers and responsibilities to a Speaker from its own party, including influence over the makeup of certain standing committees. For more information, consult CRS Report 97-780, *The Speaker of the House: House Officer, Party Leader, and Representative*, by Valerie Heitshusen, and CRS Report RL30857, *Speakers of the House: Elections, 1913-2011*, by Richard S. Beth and Valerie Heitshusen.

---

[4] *Biographical Directory of the American Congress 1774-1996* (Washington: CQ Staff Directories, Inc., 1997), p. xi. This commercially published edition of the *Biographical Directory* is a continuation of earlier editions that were published under public auspices. An online, updated, version is also available at http://bioguide.congress.gov/biosearch/biosearch.asp.

[5] Robert C. Byrd, *The Senate, 1789-1989,* 4 vols., S. Doc. 100-20, 100th Cong., 1st sess. (Washington: GPO, 1988-1993), vol. 4, *Historical Statistics, 1789-1992.* Hereafter cited as Byrd's *Historical Statistics.* See also, Gerald Gamm and Steven S. Smith, "Last Among Equals: The Senate's Presiding Officer," paper presented at the annual meeting of the American Political Science Association, Boston, MA, September 3-6, 1998.

Table 1. Speakers of the House of Representatives, 1789-2012

Speaker	Party	State	Congress	Dates
Frederick A.C. Muhlenberg	N/A	PA	1st	Apr. 1, 1789- Mar. 3, 1791
Jonathan Trumbull	N/A	CT	2nd	Oct. 24, 1791- Mar. 3, 1793
Frederick A.C. Muhlenberg	N/A	PA	3rd	Dec. 2, 1793- Mar. 3, 1795
Jonathan Dayton	N/A	NJ	4th-5th	Dec. 7, 1795- Mar. 3, 1799
Theodore Sedgwick	N/A	MA	6th	Dec. 2, 1799- Mar. 3, 1801
Nathaniel Macon	N/A	NC	7th-9th	Dec. 7, 1801-Mar. 3, 1807
Joseph B. Varnum	N/A	MA	10th-11th	Oct. 26, 1807- Mar. 3, 1811
Henry Clay	R(DR)[a]	KY	12th-13th	Nov. 4, 1811- Jan. 19, 1814[b]
Langdon Cheeves	R(DR)[a]	SC	13th	Jan. 19, 1814- Mar. 3, 1815
Henry Clay	R(DR)[a]	KY	14th-16th	Dec. 4, 1815- Oct. 28, 1820[c]
John W. Taylor	R(DR)[a]	NY	16th	Nov. 15, 1820- Mar. 3, 1821
Philip Barbour	R(DR)[a]	VA	17th	Dec. 4, 1821- Mar. 3, 1823
Henry Clay	R(DR)[a]	KY	18th	Dec. 3, 1823- Mar. 6, 1825[d]
John W. Taylor	R(DR)[a]	NY	19th	Dec. 5, 1825- Mar. 3, 1827
Andrew Stevenson	N/A	VA	20th	Dec. 3, 1827- Mar. 3, 1829
Andrew Stevenson	J	VA	21st-23rd	Dec. 7, 1829- June 2, 1834[e]
John Bell	N/A	TN	23rd	June 2, 1834- Mar. 3, 1835
James K. Polk	J	TN	24th-25th	Dec. 7, 1835- Mar. 3, 1839
Robert M.T. Hunter	W	WA	26th	Dec. 16, 1839- Mar. 3, 1841
John White	W	KY	27th	May 31, 1841- Mar. 3, 1843
John W. Jones	D	VA	28th	Dec. 4, 1843- Mar. 3, 1845
John W. Davis	D	IN	29th	Dec. 1, 1845- Mar. 3, 1847
Robert C. Winthrop	W	MA	30th	Dec. 6, 1847- Mar. 3, 1849
Howell Cobb	D	GA	31st	Dec. 22, 1849- Mar. 3, 1851
Linn Boyd	D	KY	32nd-33rd	Dec. 1, 1851- Mar. 3, 1855
Nathaniel P. Banks	Am[f]	MA	34th	Feb. 2, 1856- Mar. 3, 1857
James L. Orr	D	SC	35th	Dec. 7, 1857- Mar. 3, 1859
William Pennington	R	NJ	36th	Feb. 1, 1860- Mar. 3, 1861
Galusha A. Grow	R	PA	37th	July 4, 1861- Mar. 3, 1863
Schuyler Colfax	R	IN	38th-40th	Dec. 7, 1863- Mar. 3, 1869[g]
Theodore Pomeroy	R	NY	40th	Mar. 3, 1869[h]
James G. Blaine	R	ME	41st-43rd	Mar. 4, 1869- Mar. 3, 1875
Michael C. Kerr	D	IN	44th	Dec. 6, 1875- Aug. 19, 1876[i]
Samuel J. Randall	D	PA	44th-46th	Dec. 4, 1876- Mar. 3, 1881
J. Warren Keifer	R	OH	47th	Dec. 5, 1881- Mar. 3, 1883
John G. Carlisle	D	KY	48th-50th	Dec. 3, 1883- Mar. 3, 1889

Speaker	Party	State	Congress	Dates
Thomas B. Reed	R	ME	51st	Dec. 2, 1889- Mar. 3, 1891
Charles F. Crisp	D	GA	52nd-53rd	Dec. 7, 1891- Mar. 3, 1895
Thomas B. Reed	R	ME	54th-55th	Dec. 2, 1895- Mar. 3, 1899
David B. Henderson	R	IA	56th-57th	Dec. 4, 1899- Mar. 3, 1903
Joseph G. Cannon	R	IL	58th-61st	Nov. 9, 1903- Mar. 3, 1911
James B. (Champ) Clark	D	MO	62nd-65th	April 4, 1911- Mar. 3, 1919
Frederick H. Gillett	R	MA	66th-68th	May 19, 1919- Mar. 3, 1925
Nicholas Longworth	R	OH	69th-71st	Dec. 7, 1925- Mar. 3, 1931
John N. Garner	D	TX	72nd	Dec. 7, 1931- Mar. 3, 1933
Henry T. Rainey	D	IL	73rd	Mar. 9, 1933- Aug. 19, 1934[j]
Joseph W. Byrns	D	TN	74th	Jan. 3, 1935- June 4, 1936[k]
William B. Bankhead	D	AL	74th-76th	June 4, 1936- Sept. 15, 1940[l]
Sam T. Rayburn	D	TX	76th-79th	Sept. 16, 1940- Jan. 3, 1947[m]
Joseph W. Martin, Jr.	R	MA	80th	Jan. 3, 1947- Jan. 3, 1949
Sam T. Rayburn	D	TX	81st-82nd	Jan. 3, 1949- Jan. 3, 1953
Joseph W. Martin, Jr.	R	MA	83rd	Jan. 3, 1953- Jan. 3, 1955
Sam T. Rayburn	D	TX	84th-87th	Jan. 5, 1955- Nov. 16, 1961[m]
John W. McCormack	D	MA	87th-91st	Jan. 10, 1962- Jan. 3, 1971
Carl Albert	D	OK	92nd-94th	Jan. 21, 1971- Jan. 3, 1977
Thomas P. O'Neill, Jr.	D	MA	95th-99th	Jan. 4, 1977- Jan. 3, 1987
James C. Wright, Jr.	D	TX	100th-101st	Jan. 6, 1987- June 6, 1989[n]
Thomas S. Foley	D	WA	101st-103rd	June 6, 1989- Jan. 3, 1995
Newt Gingrich	R	GA	104th-105th	Jan. 4, 1995- Jan. 3, 1999
J. Dennis Hastert	R	IL	106th-109th	Jan. 6, 1999- Jan. 3, 2007
Nancy Pelosi	D	CA	110th-111th	Jan. 4, 2007- Jan. 3, 2012
John Boehner	R	OH	112th-	Jan. 5, 2011-

Sources: See the "Source Notes and Bibliography" section at the end of this report for a description and full citation of all sources.

Notes: A key to all party abbreviations can be found in the **Appendix** of this report.

a. Although the *Biographical Directory of the American Congress, 1774-1996* identifies these Speakers as Republicans, the party designation "Democratic Republicans" is more widely used and familiar to readers. This designation, R(DR), should not be taken to refer to the contemporary Republican Party, which did not emerge until the 1850s.

b. Resigned from the House of Representatives, January 19, 1814.

c. Resigned the Speakership on October 28, 1820.

d. Resigned from the House, March 6, 1825.

e. Resigned from the House, June 2, 1834.

f. Speaker Nathaniel P. Banks served in the House three separate times under three different party designations. In the 34th Congress, he served as an American Party Member.

g. Resigned from the House, March 3, 1869.

h. Elected Speaker, March 3, 1869, and served one day.

i. Died in office, August 19, 1876.

j. Died in office, August 19, 1934.

k. Died in office, June 4, 1936.

l. Died in office, September 15, 1940.

m. Died in office, November 16, 1961.

n. Resigned the Speakership, June 6, 1989; resigned from the House, June 30, 1989.

Party Floor Leader

At an organizational meeting prior to the beginning of a new Congress, each party conference (or caucus) in the House selects its floor leader (also called majority leader or minority leader, as appropriate) in a secret-ballot vote. The majority party floor leader works closely with the Speaker and is largely responsible for the party's daily legislative operations, in consultation with other party leaders. Similarly, the minority party floor leader directs the party's ongoing legislative strategies and operations and typically serves as the spokesperson for the party in the House. Each party assigns additional responsibilities to its respective floor leader. For more information on the majority party floor leader position, see CRS Report RL30665, *The Role of the House Majority Leader: An Overview*, by Walter J. Oleszek.

Table 2. House Republican Floor Leaders, 1899-2012

Floor Leader	State	Congress	Dates
Sereno E. Payne	NY	56th-61st	1899-1911
James R. Mann	IL	62nd-65th	1911-1919
Franklin W. Mondell	WY	66th-67th	1919-1923
Nicholas Longworth	OH	68th	1923-1925
John Q. Tilson	CT	69th-71st	1925-1931
Bertrand H. Snell	NY	72nd-75th	1931-1939
Joseph W. Martin, Jr.	MA	76th-79th	1939-1947
Charles Halleck	IN	80th	1947-1949
Joseph W. Martin, Jr.	MA	81st-82nd	1949-1953
Charles Halleck	IN	83rd	1953-1955
Joseph W. Martin, Jr.	MA	84th-85th	1955-1959
Charles Halleck	IN	86th-88th	1959-1965
Gerald R. Ford	MI	89th-93rd	1965-Dec. 6, 1973[a]
John J. Rhodes	AZ	93rd-96th	Dec. 7, 1973-1981
Robert H. Michel	IL	97th-103rd	1981-1995
Richard K. Armey	TX	104th-107th	1995-2003
Tom DeLay	TX	108th-109th	2003-Sept. 28, 2005[b]
Roy Blunt	MO	109th	Sept. 28, 2005-Feb. 2, 2006[c]

Floor Leader	State	Congress	Dates
John Boehner	OH	**109**th, 110th-111th	Feb. 2, 2006-2011
Eric Cantor	VA	**112**th	2011-

Sources: See the "Source Notes and Bibliography" section at the end of this report for a description and full citation of all sources.

Notes: Bolded entries indicate Congresses in which the floor leader was also majority leader.

a. Resigned from the House on December 6, 1973, after having been confirmed by the Senate to become Vice President to fill the post vacated by the resignation of Spiro T. Agnew.

b. Resigned from leader position on September 28, 2005.

c. Appointed acting Republican floor leader on September 28, 2005, to replace Tom DeLay temporarily until the conference could hold new elections on February 2, 2006. He continued serving as Republican Whip during this period.

Table 3. House Democratic Floor Leaders, 1899-2012

Floor Leader	State	Congress	Dates
James D. Richardson	TN	56th-57th	1899-1903
John Sharp Williams	MS	58th-60th	1903-1908
James B. (Champ) Clark	MO	60th-61st	1908-1911
Oscar W. Underwood	AL	62nd-63rd	1911-1915
Claude Kitchin	NC	**64**th-**65**th	1915-1919
James B. (Champ) Clark	MO	66th	1919-1921
Claude Kitchin	NC	67th	1921-1923
Finis J. Garrett	IN	68th-70th	1923-1929
John N. Garner	TX	71st	1929-1931
Henry T. Rainey	IL	**72**nd	1931-1933
Joseph W. Byrns	TN	**73**rd	1933-1935
William B. Bankhead	AL	**74**th	1935-June 4, 1936[a]
Sam T. Rayburn	TX	**75**th-**76**th	1937-Sept. 16, 1940[b]
John W. McCormack	MA	**76**th-**79**th	Sept. 16, 1940-1947[c]
Sam T. Rayburn	TX	80th	1947-1949
John W. McCormack	MA	**81**st-**82**nd	1949-1953
Sam T. Rayburn	TX	83rd	1953-1955
John W. McCormack	MA	**84**th-**87**th	1955-Jan. 10, 1962[d]
Carl Albert	OK	**87**th-**91**st	Jan. 10, 1962-1971[e]
Thomas Hale Boggs	LA	**92**nd	1971-1973[f]
Thomas P. O'Neill, Jr.	MA	**93**rd-**94**th	1973-1977
James Wright	TX	**95**th-**99**th	1977-1987
Thomas S. Foley	WA	**100**th-**101**st	1987-June 6, 1989[g]
Richard A. Gephardt	MO	**101**st-**103**rd 104th-107th	June 14, 1989[h]-2003

Floor Leader	State	Congress	Dates
Nancy Pelosi	CA	108th-109th	2003-2007
Steny H. Hoyer	MD	**110th-111th**	2007-2011
Nancy Pelosi	CA	112th	2011-

Sources: See the "Source Notes and Bibliography" section at the end of this report for a description and full citation of all sources.

Notes: Bolded entries indicate Congresses in which the floor leader was also majority leader.

a. Elected Speaker, filling the vacancy caused by the death of Speaker Joseph W. Byrns. Records indicate that Representative John J. O'Connor of New York, chair of the House Rules Committee, served as acting majority leader during the 14 remaining days of the 74th Congress. O'Connor does not, however, appear to have been formally elected majority leader at that time and therefore is not included in this list.

b. Elected Speaker following the death of Speaker William B. Bankhead.

c. Elected majority leader on September 16, 1940, to fill post made vacant by the election of Sam Rayburn as Speaker.

d. Elected Speaker at the start of the 87th Congress, 2nd session, following the death of Sam Rayburn.

e. Elected majority leader at commencement of the 87th Congress, 2nd session, when Majority Leader John McCormack was elected Speaker to succeed Speaker Rayburn.

f. Disappeared on a flight from Anchorage to Juneau, Alaska, October 16, 1972. Presumed dead pursuant to House Resolution 1, 93rd Congress.

g. Elected Speaker on June 6, 1989, following Speaker James C. Wright's resignation from that post on the same date.

h. Elected majority leader on June 14, 1989, to fill the post made vacant by the election of Thomas S. Foley to be Speaker on June 6, 1989.

Party Whip

Each House party caucus currently elects its own party whip at organizational meetings as a new Congress begins. House Republicans (or a representative group of their conference) have always elected their party whips; Democrats in the House appointed a chief whip until 1986. Chief deputy whips are currently appointed by the party's chief whip; additional members to serve in the whip team are either similarly appointed or, instead, elected by subsets of the caucus. The whip organization is responsible for assessing the passage prospects for upcoming measures, mobilizing member support for leadership priorities, informing the party rank-and-file regarding legislative scheduling and initiatives, and informing the top party leadership regarding the sentiment of the rank-and-file. For more information, see CRS Report RS20499, *House Leadership: Whip Organization*, by Judy Schneider.

Table 4. House Democratic Whips, 1901-2012

Whip	State	Congress	Dates
Oscar W. Underwood[a]	AL	56th	1901
James T. Lloyd	MO	57th-60th	1901-1908[b]
N/A[c]		61st-**62nd**	1909-1913
Thomas M. Bell	GA	**63rd**	1913-1915
N/A[c]		**64th-65th**, 66th	1915-1921

Whip	State	Congress	Dates
William A. Oldfield	AR	67th-70th	1921-Nov. 19, 1928[d]
John McDuffie	AL	70th-71st, **72nd**	1928-1933
Arthur Greenwood	IN	**73rd**	1933-1935
Patrick J. Boland	PA	**74th-77th**	1935-May 18, 1942[e]
Robert Ramspeck	GA	**77th-79th**	1942-Dec. 31, 1945[f]
John J. Sparkman	AL	**79th**	1946-1947
John W. McCormack[a]	MA	80th	1947-1949
J. Percy Priest	TN	**81st-82nd**	1949-1953
John W. McCormack[a]	MA	83rd	1953-1955
Carl Albert[a]	OK	**84th-87th**	1955-1962
Thomas Hale Boggs[a]	LA	**87th-91st**	1962-1971
Thomas P. O'Neill, Jr.[a]	MA	**92nd**	1971-1973
John J. McFall	CA	**93rd-94th**	1973-1977
John W. Brademas	IN	**95th-96th**	1977-1981
Thomas S. Foley[a]	WA	**97th-99th**	1981-1987
Tony Coelho[g]	CA	**100th-101st**	1987-June 14, 1989
William H. Gray, III	PA	**101st-102nd**	June 14, 1989-Sept. 11, 1991[h]
David E. Bonior	MI	**102nd-103rd** 104th-107th	Sept. 11, 1991-Jan. 15, 2002[i]
Nancy Pelosi[a]	CA	107th-108th	Jan. 15, 2002-2003[j]
Steny H. Hoyer[a]	MD	108th -109th	2003-2007
James E. Clyburn	SC	**110th-111th**	2007-2011
Steny H. Hoyer	MD	112th	2011-

Sources: See the "Source Notes and Bibliography" section at the end of this report for a description and full citation of all sources.

Notes: Bolded entries indicate Congresses in which the Democratic whip was the majority whip.

a. Ascended (or re-ascended) to party floor leader.

b. Resigned from position as Democratic whip in 1908 at the conclusion of the 60th Congress.

c. For these periods, there is no official record—in the minutes of the Democratic Caucus or elsewhere—of the name of the Democratic whip. Some scholars believe that Representative Thomas Bell may have been the whip from 1909 to 1919; others believe the whip for that period may have been Representative John Nance Garner. See Randall B. Ripley, "The Party Whip Organizations in the United States House of Representatives," *American Political Science Review,* vol. 58, September 1964, p. 504.

d. Died in office, November 19, 1928.

e. Died in office, May 18, 1942.

f. Resigned from the House of Representatives, December 31, 1945.

g. Representative Tony Coelho was the first elected Democratic whip.

h. Resigned from the House of Representatives, September 11, 1991.

i. Elected July 11, 1991, but did not assume the House Democratic whip post until his predecessor in the position, William H. Gray, III, resigned from Congress on September 11, 1991.

j. Elected on October 10, 2001, but did not assume the position of House Democratic whip until January 15, 2002, the date on which Bonior's resignation as whip became effective.

Table 5. House Republican Whips, 1897-2012

Whip	State	Congress	Dates
James A. Tawney	MN	**55th-58th**	1897-1905
James E. Watson	IN	**59th-60th**	1905-1909
John W. Dwight	NY	61st 62nd	1909-1913
Charles H. Burke	SD	63rd	1913-1915
Charles M. Hamilton	WY	64th-65th	1915-1919
Harold Knutson	MN	**66th-67th**	1919-1923
Albert H. Vestal	IN	**68th-71st**	1923-1931
Carl G. Bachmann	WV	72nd	1931-1933
Harry L. Englebright	CA	73rd-78th	1933-May 13, 1943[a]
Leslie C. Arends	IL	78th-79th **80th** 81st-82nd **83rd** 84th-93rd	1943-1975
Robert H. Michel[b]	IL	94th-96th	1975-1981
Trent Lott	MS	97th-100th	1981-1989
Dick Cheney	WY	101st	1989-Mar. 17, 1989[c]
Newt Gingrich	GA	101st-103rd	Mar. 22, 1989-1995[c]
Tom DeLay[b]	TX	**104th-107th**	1995-2003
Roy D. Blunt[b]	MO	**108th-109th** 110th	2003[d]-2009
Eric Cantor[b]	VA	111th	2009-2011
Kevin McCarthy	CA	**112th-**	2011-

Sources: See the "Source Notes and Bibliography" section at the end of this report for a description and full citation of all sources.

Notes: Bolded entries indicate Congresses in which the Republican whip was the majority whip.

a. Died in office, May 13, 1943.

b. Ascended to party floor leader.

c. Elected House Republican whip on March 22, 1989, following Representative Dick Cheney's resignation from the House on March 17, 1989, to become Secretary of Defense.

d. Served concurrently as whip and acting Republican floor leader from September 28, 2005, to February 2, 2006.

Conference or Caucus Chair

The Republican Conference and the Democratic Caucus are the organizations of the members of the respective parties in the House. Each conference has an elected chair, who presides over its meetings. Decisions made by the conference (and often publicly promulgated by the chair) are generally regarded as the collective sentiment of the respective House party contingent.

Table 6. House Republican Conference Chairs, 1863-2012

Chair	State	Congress	Dates
Justin S. Morrill[a]	VT	38th-39th	1863-1867
N/A[b]		40th	1867-1869
Robert C. Schenck[c]	OH	41st	1869-1871
Nathaniel P. Banks[c]	MA		
Austin Blair	MI	42nd	1871-1873
Horace Maynard	TN	43rd	1873-1875
George W. McCrary	IA	44th	1875-1877
Eugene Hale	ME	45th	1877-1879
William P. Frye	ME	46th	1879-1881
G.M. Robeson	NJ	47th	1881-1883
Joseph G. Cannon	IL	48th-50th	1883-1889
T.J. Henderson	IL	51st 52nd-53rd	1889-1895
Charles H. Grosvenor	OH	54th-55th	1895-1899
Joseph G. Cannon	IL	56th-57th	1899-1903
William P. Hepburn	IA	58th-60th	1903-1909
F.D. Currier	NH	61st 62nd	1909-1913
William S. Greene	MA	63rd-65th	1913-1919
Horace M. Towner	IA	66th-67th	1919-1923
Sydney Anderson	MN	68th	1923-1925
Willis C. Hawley	OR	69th-71st 72nd	1925-1933
Robert Luce	MA	73rd	1933-1935
Frederick R. Lehlbach	NJ	74th	1935-1937
Roy Woodruff	MI	75th-79th 80th 81st	1937-1951
Clifford Hope	KS	82nd 83rd 84th	1951-1957
Charles Hoeven	IA	85th-87th	1957-1963
Gerald R. Ford	MI	88th	1963-1965
Melvin Laird	WI	89th-90th	1965-1969
John B. Anderson	IL	91st-95th	1969-1979
Samuel L. Devine	OH	96th	1979-1981
Jack Kemp	NY	97th-99th	1981-June 4, 1987[d]
Dick Cheney	WY	100th	June 4, 1987-1989[d]
Jerry Lewis	CA	101st-102nd	1989-1993

Chair	State	Congress	Dates
Richard K. Armey	TX	103rd	1993-1995
John A. Boehner	OH	**104th-105th**	1995-1999
J.C. Watts	OK	**106th-107th**	1999-2003
Deborah Pryce	OH	**108th-109th**	2003-2007
Adam Putnam	FL	110th	2007-2009
Mike Pence	IN	111th	2009-2011
Jeb Hensarling	TX	**112th-**	2011-

Sources: See the "Source Notes and Bibliography" section at the end of this report for a description and full citation of all sources.

Notes: Bolded entries indicate Congresses in which the Republican Party was in the majority.

a. Representative Justin S. Morrill is the first officially designated Republican caucus chair. There exists no clear evidence of formal chairs of Republican organizations in earlier Congresses.

b. Caucus minutes show three Members (Representatives Nathaniel Banks, Luke Poland, and Samuel Hooper) chairing three separate meetings.

c. Caucus minutes show Representative Robert C. Schenck elected chair, but Representative Nathaniel P. Banks chairing two early meetings, possibly in Schenck's absence.

d. On June 4, 1987, Representative Dick Cheney was elected conference chair to succeed Representative Jack Kemp, who resigned from the post.

Table 7. House Democratic Caucus Chairs, 1849-2012

Chair	State	Congress	Dates
James Thompson	PA	31st	1849-1851
N/A[a]		32nd	1851-1853
Edson B. Olds	OH	33rd	1853-1855
George W. Jones	TN	34th	1855-1857
N/A[b]		**35th**	1857-1859
George S. Houston	AL	36th	1859-1861
N/A[c]		37th-40th	1861-1869
William E. Niblack[d] Samuel J. Randall[d]	IN PA	41st	1869-1871
N/A[e]		42nd	1871-1873
William E. Niblack	IN	43rd	1873-1875
Lucius Q.C. Lamar	MS	**44th**	1875-1877
Hiester Clymer	PA	**45th**	1877-1879
John F. House	TN	**46th**	1879-1881
N/A[f]		47th	1881-1883
George W. Geddes	OH	**48th**	1883-1885
J. Randolph Tucker	VA	**49th**	1885-1887
Samuel S. Cox	NY	**50th**	1887-1889[g]

Chair	State	Congress	Dates
William S. Holman	IN	51st **52nd-53rd**	1889-1895
David B. Culberson	TX	54th	1895-1897
James D. Richardson	TN	55th	1897-1899
James Hay	VA	56th-58th	1899-1905
Robert L. Henry	TX	59th	1905-1907
Henry D. Clayton	AL	60th-61st	1907-1911[h]
Albert S. Burleson	TX	**62nd**	1911-1913[h]
A. Mitchell Palmer	PA	**63rd**	1913-1915
E.W. Saunders	VA	**64th-65th**	1915-1919
Arthur G. Dewalt	PA	66th	1919-1921
Sam T. Rayburn	TX	67th	1921-1923
Henry T. Rainey	IL	68th	1923-1925
Charles D. Carter	OK	69th	1925-1927
Arthur Greenwood	IN	70th	1927-1929
David Kincheloe	KY	71st	1929-1930[i]
William W. Arnold	IL	**72nd**	1931-1933
Clarence F. Lea	CA	**73rd**	1933-1935
Edward T. Taylor	CO	**74th**	1935-1937
Robert L. Doughton	NC	**75th**	1937-1939
John W. McCormack	MA	**76th**	1939-Sept. 16, 1940[j]
Richard M. Duncan	MO	**77th**	1941-1943
Harry Sheppard	CA	**78th**	1943-1945
Jere Cooper	TN	**79th**	1945-1947
Aime Forand	RI	80th	1947-1949
Francis E. Walter	PA	**81st**	1949-1951
Jere Cooper	TN	**82nd**	1951-1953
Wilbur Mills	AR	83rd	1953-1955
John J. Rooney	NY	**84th**	1955-1957
Melvin Price	IL	**85th-86th**	1957-1961
Francis E. Walter	PA	**87th-88th**	1961-May 31, 1963[k]
Albert Thomas	TX	**88th**	1964-1965
Eugene Keogh	NY	**89th**	1965-1967
Dan Rostenkowski	IL	**90th-91st**	1967-1971
Olin Teague	TX	**92nd-93rd**	1971-1975
Philip Burton	CA	**94th**	1975-1977
Thomas S. Foley	WA	**95th-96th**	1977-1981

Chair	State	Congress	Dates
Gillis W. Long	LA	**97th-98th**	1981-1985
Richard Gephardt	MO	**99th-100th**	1985-1989
William H. Gray, III	PA	**101st**	Jan. 4-June 14, 1989[l]
Steny H. Hoyer	MD	**101st-103rd**	June 21, 1989-1995[m]
Vic Fazio	CA	104th-105th	1995-1999
Martin Frost	TX	106th-107th	1999-2003
Robert Menendez	NJ	108th-109th	2003-Dec. 16, 2005[n]
James E. Clyburn	SC	109th	Dec. 16, 2005[n]-2007
Rahm Emanuel	IL	110th	2007-2009
John B. Larson	CT	111th-	2009-

Sources: See the "Source Notes and Bibliography" section at the end of this report for a description and full citation of all sources.

Notes: Bolded entries indicate Congresses in which the Democratic Party was in the majority.

a. No clear records remain for this Congress. In early practice, the caucus chair often offered the various organizational resolutions at the beginning of a Congress (e.g., the nomination of his party's candidate for Speaker, or the motion to elect the Speaker); examination of these motions can often help in a determination of who was caucus chair. However, several different Democratic Members offered the organizing resolutions for the 31st Congress.

b. No clear data for this period exist.

c. No clear data for this period exist. Representative John Hickman nominated Representative F.P. Blair as Speaker in 1861, but no records show whether Hickman was caucus chair.

d. Representative Samuel J. Randall nominated the party's candidate for Speaker. Caucus records, however, show both Representatives William B. Niblack and Randall as having served as chair during the Congress. The caucus records specify no dates of service.

e. Representative Fernando Wood nominated the Democratic leadership slate in the House, but there is no other evidence to show he was elected caucus chair.

f. Available data show that Representative John F. House offered the Democrats' nomination for Speaker in the 47th Congress. However, later data show Representative W.S. Rosecrans issuing the next call for a Democratic Caucus meeting; there is no evidence to suggest that Rosecrans was actually elected caucus chair.

g. Former Parliamentarian Clarence Cannon's notes state that "[Representative Samuel J.] Cox died during this Congress and [Representative James B.] McCreary evidently succeeded or acted for him." Representative Cox died on September 10, 1889, six months after the sine die adjournment of the 50th Congress and the convening of the 51st Congress.

h. Caucus records are contradictory for this period. They show the election of Representative James Hay as chair on January 19, 1911, but do not mention a resignation by incumbent chair Henry P. Clayton, nor do they specify that Hay was elected chair for the new Congress. Later, they show the election of Representative Albert S. Burleson on April 11, 1911.

i. Resigned from the House, October 5, 1930; there is no record of an election to fill the vacancy as caucus chair.

j. Resigned following election as majority floor leader, September 16, 1940; records do not indicate that a successor was chosen during the remainder of the Congress.

k. Died in office, May 31, 1963. Caucus chair post vacant until January 21, 1964.

l. Representative William H. Gray, III, vacated the caucus chair post when he was elected Democratic whip on June 14, 1989.

m.   Representative Steny H. Hoyer was elected caucus chair on June 21, 1989, following the June 14, 1989 election of Representative William H. Gray as Democratic whip.

n.   Representative Robert Menendez resigned from the House on January 16, 2006, after being apppointed to the Senate seat for New Jersey vacated by Jon Corzine when he was elected governor. Representative Menendez had previously resigned from the caucus chair position, to which Representative James E. Clyburn was elected on December 16, 2005.

Senate Positions: Descriptions and Historical Tables

President Pro Tempore of the Senate

Pursuant to Article 1, Section 3, of the U.S. Constitution, the President pro tempore of the Senate is the chamber's presiding officer in the absence of the President of the Senate (the Vice President of the United States). The President pro tempore is elected by the full Senate as the formal institutional leader, and in current practice, is the longest-serving member of the majority party.[6] Until 1890, the Senate elected a President pro tempore whenever the Vice President was not in attendance, whether for a day, or permanently, as in the case of the Vice President's death or resignation. When the Vice President returned, the President pro tempore lost his place. When the Vice President was again absent, the Senate again elected a President pro tempore—in many cases the same Senator who had been chosen before. By the standing order agreed to on March 12, 1890, the Senate declared that the President pro tempore shall hold the office during "the pleasure of the Senate and until another is elected, and shall execute the duties thereof during all future absences of the Vice President until the Senate does otherwise order."[7]

The Senate's President pro tempore is, pursuant to statute, currently third in the line of presidential succession (behind the Vice President and the Speaker of the House). In the Succession Act of 1792, the position was initially designated to serve in line after the Vice President.[8] An 1886 act altered the succession line by replacing congressional leaders with cabinet secretaries, but the President pro tempore post was reinstated in the line (in the current position) in 1947.[9]

As presiding officer, the President pro tempore has the power to decide points of order and enforce decorum on the floor. The President pro tempore has other formal powers (e.g., appointing conferees; appointing certain Senate officers; and serving on, or appointing others to, working groups, commissions, and advisory boards); however, because the direction of Senate business has fallen in modern times to the majority leader, almost all of these powers are actually exercised by the majority leader in practice.

As explained in the notes to **Table 9** and **Table 10** below, the Senate has also had past occasion to select a Deputy President pro tempore and a Permanent Acting President pro tempore. For more information on the President pro tempore (and the deputy and acting posts), consult CRS Report

---

[6] Electing the longest-serving majority party Senator has generally been the practice since 1890, with some exceptions. The only exception since 1945 has been the election of Senator Arthur Vandenberg in 1947.

[7] U.S. Congress, Senate Journal, 50th Cong., 2nd sess., p. 165. See also "President Pro Tempore of the Senate," *Congressional Record*, vol. 21 (March 12, 1890), pp. 2144-2150.

[8] 1 Stat. 240.

[9] 24 Stat 1; 61 Stat. 380.

RL30960, *The President Pro Tempore of the Senate: History and Authority of the Office*, by Christopher M. Davis.

Table 8. Presidents Pro Tempore of the Senate, 1789-2012

Name	Party	State	Congress	Date Elected
John Langdon	Pro-Admin	NH	1st	Apr. 6, 1789
Richard Henry Lee	Anti-Admin	VA	2nd	Apr. 18, 1792
John Langdon	Pro-Admin	NH	2nd	Nov. 5, 1792
				Mar. 1, 1793
Ralph Izard	Pro-Admin	SC	3rd	May 31, 1794
Henry Tazewell	Anti-Admin	VA	3rd	Feb. 20, 1795
	R(DR)[a]		4th	Dec. 7, 1795
Samuel Livermore	F	NH	4th	May 6, 1796
William Bingham	F	PA	4th	Feb. 16, 1797
William Bradford	F	RI	5th	July 6, 1797
Jacob Read	F	SC	5th	Nov. 22, 1797
Theodore Sedgwick	F	MA	5th	June 27, 1798
John Laurance	F	NY	5th	Dec. 6, 1798
James Ross	F	PA	5th	Mar. 1, 1799
Samuel Livermore	F	NH	6th	Dec. 22, 1799
Uriah Tracy	F	CT	6th	May 14, 1800
John E. Howard	F	MD	6th	Nov. 21, 1800
James Hillhouse	F	CT	6th	Feb. 28, 1801
Abraham Baldwin	R	GA	7th	Dec. 7, 1801
Stephen R. Bradley	R(DR)[a]	VT	7th	Dec. 14, 1802
				Feb. 25, 1803
				Mar. 2, 1803
John Brown	Anti-Admin	KY	8th	Oct. 17, 1803
				Jan. 23, 1804
Jesse Franklin	R(DR)[a]	NC	8th	Mar. 10, 1804
Joseph Anderson	R(DR)[a]	TN	8th	Jan. 15, 1805
				Feb. 28, 1805
				Mar. 2, 1805
Samuel Smith	R(DR)[a]	MD	9th	Dec. 2, 1805
			10th	Mar. 18, 1806
				Mar. 2, 1807
				Apr. 16, 1808
Stephen R. Bradley	R(DR)[a]	VT	10th	Dec. 28, 1808

Name	Party	State	Congress	Date Elected
John Milledge	R(DR)[a]	GA	10th	Jan. 30, 1809
Andrew Gregg	R(DR)[a]	PA	11th	June 26, 1809
John Gaillard	R(DR)[a]	SC	11th	Feb. 28, 1810
				Apr. 17, 1810
John Pope	R(DR)[a]	KY	11th	Feb. 23, 1811
William H. Crawford	R(DR)[a]	GA	12th	Mar. 24, 1812
Joseph B. Varnum	R(DR)[a]	MA	13th	Dec. 6, 1813
John Gaillard	R(DR)[a]	SC	13th	Apr. 18, 1814
			14th	Nov. 25, 1814[b]
			15th	[no election]
				Mar. 6, 1817
				Mar. 31, 1918
James Barbour	R(DR)[a]	VA	15th	Feb. 15, 1819
			16th	[no election]
John Gaillard	R(DR)[a]	SC	16th	Jan. 25, 1820
			17th	Feb. 1, 1822
			18th	Feb. 19, 1823
	CRR J		19th	May 21, 1824
				Mar. 9, 1825
Nathaniel Macon	J	NC	19th	May 20, 1826
				Jan. 2, 1827
				Mar. 2, 1827
Samuel Smith	J	MD	20th	May 15, 1828
			21st	Mar. 13, 1829
				May 29, 1830
				Mar. 1, 1831
Littleton Tazewell	J	VA	22nd	July 9, 1832
Hugh L. White	J	TN	22nd	Dec. 3, 1832
			23rd	[no election]
George Poindexter	AJ	MS	23rd	June 28, 1834
John Tyler	AJ	VA	23rd	Mar. 3, 1835
William R. King	J	AL	24th	July 1, 1836
	D		25th	Jan. 28, 1837
			26th	Mar. 7, 1837
			27th	Oct. 13, 1837
				July 2, 1838
				Feb. 25, 1839

Name	Party	State	Congress	Date Elected
				July 3, 1840
				Mar. 3, 1841
				Mar. 4, 1841
Samuel Southard	W	NJ	27th	Mar. 11, 1841
Willie P. Mangum	W	NC	27th	May 31, 1842
			28th	[no election]
Ambrose H. Sevier	D	AR	29th	Dec. 27, 1845c
David R. Atchison	D	MO	29th	Aug. 8, 1846
			30th	Jan. 11, 1847
			31st	Mar. 3, 1847
				Feb. 2, 1848
				June 1, 1848
				June 26, 1848
				July 29, 1848
				Dec. 26, 1848
				Mar. 2, 1849
				Mar. 5, 1849
				Mar. 16, 1849
William R. King	D	AL	31st	May 6, 1850
			32nd	July 11, 1850
				[no election]
David R. Atchison	D	MO	32nd	Dec. 20, 1852 Mar. 4, 1853
			33rd	
Lewis Cass	D	MI	33rd	Dec. 4, 1854
Jesse D. Bright	D	IN	33rd	Dec. 5, 1854
			34th	June 11, 1856
Charles E. Stuart	D	MI	34th	June 9, 1856
James M. Mason	D	VA	34th	Jan. 6, 1857
			35th	Mar. 4, 1857
Thomas J. Rusk	D	TX	35th	Mar. 14, 1857
Benjamin Fitzpatrick	D	AL	35th	Dec. 7, 1857
			36th	Mar. 29, 1858
				June 14, 1858
				Jan. 25, 1858
				Mar. 9, 1859
				Dec. 19, 1859
				Feb. 20, 1860

Name	Party	State	Congress	Date Elected
Jesse D. Bright	D	IN	36th	June 12, 1860
Benjamin Fitzpatrick	D	AL	36th	June 26, 1860
Solomon Foot	R	VT	36th	Feb. 16, 1861
			37th	Mar. 23, 1861
			38th	July 18, 1861
				Jan. 15, 1862
				Mar. 31, 1862
				June 19, 1862
				Feb. 18, 1863
				Mar. 4, 1863
				Dec. 18, 1863
				Feb. 23, 1864
				Apr. 11, 1864
Daniel Clark	R	NH	38th	Apr. 26, 1864
				Feb. 9, 1865
Lafayette S. Foster	R	CT	39th	Mar. 7, 1865
Benjamin F. Wade	R	OH	39th	Mar. 2, 1867
			40th	[no election]
Henry B. Anthony	R	RI	41st	Mar. 23, 1869
			42nd	Apr. 9, 1869
				May 28, 1870
				July 1, 1870
				July 14, 1870
				Mar. 10, 1871
				Apr. 17, 1871
				May 23, 1871
				Dec. 21, 1871
				Feb. 23, 1872
				June 8, 1872
				Dec. 4, 1872
				Dec. 13, 1872
				Dec. 20, 1872
				Jan. 24, 1873
Matthew H. Carpenter	R	WI	43rd	Mar. 12, 1873
				Mar. 26, 1873
				Dec. 11, 1873
				Dec. 23, 1874

Name	Party	State	Congress	Date Elected
Henry B. Anthony	R	RI	43rd	Jan. 25, 1875
				Feb. 15, 1875
Thomas W. Ferry	R	MI	44th	Mar. 9, 1875
			45th	Mar. 19, 1875
				Dec. 20, 1875
				Mar. 5, 1877
				Feb. 26, 1878
				Apr. 17, 1878
				Mar. 3, 1879
Allen G. Thurman	D	OH	46th	Apr. 15, 1879
				Apr. 7, 1880
				May 6, 1880
Thomas F. Bayard, Sr.	D	DE	47th	Oct. 10, 1881
David Davis	I	IL	47th	Oct. 13, 1881
George F. Edmonds	R	VT	47th	Mar. 3, 1883
			48th	Jan. 14, 1884
John Sherman	R	OH	49th	Dec. 7, 1885
John J. Ingalls	R	KS	49th	Feb. 25, 1887
			50th	[no election]
			51st	Mar. 7, 1889
				Apr. 2, 1889
				Feb. 28, 1890
				Apr. 3, 1890[d]
Charles F. Manderson	R	NE	51st-53rd	Mar. 2, 1891
Isham G. Harris	D	TN	53rd	Mar. 22, 1893
Matt W. Ransom	D	NC	53rd	Jan. 7, 1895
Isham G. Harris	D	TN	53rd	Jan. 10, 1895
William P. Frye	R	ME	54th-56th	Feb. 7, 1896
			57th-59th	Mar. 7, 1901
			60th-62nd	Dec. 5, 1907
Charles Curtis	R	KS	62nd	Dec. 4, 1911
Augustus O. Bacon	D	GA	62nd	Jan. 15, 1912
Jacob H. Gallinger	R	NH	62nd	Feb. 12, 1912
Henry Cabot Lodge, Sr.	R	MA	62nd	Mar. 25, 1912
Frank B. Brandegee	R	CT	62nd	May 25, 1912
James P. Clarke	D	AR	63rd	Mar. 13, 1913
			64th	Dec. 6, 1915

Name	Party	State	Congress	Date Elected
Willard Saulsbury, Jr.	D	DE	64th-65th	Dec. 14, 1916
Albert B. Cummins	R	IA	66th	May 19, 1919
			67th-69th	Mar. 7, 1921
George H. Moses	R	NH	69th	Mar. 6, 1925
			70th-72nd	Dec. 15, 1927
Key Pittman	D	NV	73rd	Mar. 9, 1933
			74th-76th	Jan. 7, 1935
William H. King	D	UT	76th	Nov. 19, 1940
Pat Harrison	D	MS	77th	Jan. 6, 1941
Carter Glass	D	VA	77th	July 10, 1941
			78th	Jan. 5, 1943
Kenneth D. McKellar	D	TN	79th	Jan. 6, 1945
Arthur Vandenberg	R	MI	80th	Jan. 4, 1947
Kenneth D. McKellar	D	TN	81st-82nd	Jan. 3, 1949
Styles Bridges	R	NH	83rd	Jan. 3, 1953
Walter F. George	D	GA	84th	Jan. 5, 1955
Carl T. Hayden	D	AZ	85th-90th	Jan. 3, 1957
Richard B. Russell, Jr.	D	GA	91st-92nd	Jan. 3, 1969
Allen J. Ellender	D	LA	92nd	Jan. 22, 1971
James O. Eastland	D	MS	92nd-95th	July 28, 1972
Warren G. Magnuson	D	WA	96th	Jan. 15, 1979
Milton R. Young	R	ND	96th	Dec. 4, 1980
Strom Thurmond	R	SC	97th-99th	Jan. 5, 1981
John C. Stennis	D	MS	100th	Jan. 6, 1987
Robert C. Byrd	D	WV	101st-103rd	Jan. 3, 1989
Strom Thurmond	R	SC	104th-106th	Jan. 4, 1995
Robert C. Byrd	D	WV	107th	Jan. 3, 2001[e]
Strom Thurmond	R	SC	107th	Jan. 3, 2001[e]
Robert C. Byrd[f]	D	WV	107th	June 6, 2001
Ted Stevens	R	AK	108th-109th	Jan. 7, 2003
Robert C. Byrd	D	WV	110th-111th	Jan. 4, 2007[g]
Daniel K. Inouye	D	HI	111th-112th	June 28, 2010 [h]
Patrick J. Leahy	D	VT	112th-	Dec. 17, 2012

Sources: The principal source for this table is Byrd's *Historical Statistics*, pp. 647-653. See the "Source Notes and Bibliography" section at the end of this report for a description and full citation of all sources.

Notes: A key to party abbreviations can be found in the **Appendix** of this report. Note that several Senators holding the President pro tempore position were members of (or identified with) different political parties during their congressional careers. This table lists the party with which each individual was affiliated at the time of his service as President pro tempore. In cases in which the historical sources indicate a party "switch" in the midst of a calendar year (without a specific date), it is presumed that the party switch coincided with the beginning of a new Congress.

a. Although the *Biographical Directory of the American Congress, 1774-1996* identifies these Presidents pro tempore as Republicans, the party designation "Democratic Republicans" is more widely used and familiar to readers. This designation, R(DR), should not be taken to refer to the contemporary Republican Party, which did not emerge until the 1850s.

b. Senator John Gaillard was elected after the death of Vice President Elbridge Gerry on November 23, 1814, and continued to serve throughout the 14th Congress, as there was no Vice President.

c. There was no actual election. Senator Ambrose H. Sevier was "permitted to occupy the chair for the day." In their table of Presidents pro tempore, Gerald Gamm and Steven S. Smith do not include Sevier's service. See Gerald Gamm and Steven S. Smith, "Last Among Equals," "Table 1: Presidents Pro Tempore of the Senate," p.13.

d. As noted above, in March 1890, the Senate adopted a resolution stating that Presidents pro tempore would hold office continuously until the election of another President pro tempore, rather than being elected only for the period in which the Vice President was absent. That system has continued to the present.

e. When the 107th Congress convened on January 3, 2001, Republican George W. Bush had been elected President. Richard B. Cheney, Vice President-elect, would not be sworn in until January 20, 2001. As a consequence, the Senate was evenly divided, 50 Democrats and 50 Republicans. When Congress convened on January 3, 2001, Vice President Al Gore, a Democrat, remained as President of the Senate, providing Senate Democrats with an effective majority of one. On January 3, 2001, the Senate adopted S.Res. 3, which provided for the election of Senator Robert C. Byrd, Democrat of West Virginia, to serve as President pro tempore from January 3 until the inauguration of President Bush and Vice President Cheney at noon on January 20, at which time Senator Strom Thurmond, Republican of South Carolina, would assume the office of President pro tempore. See "Election of the Honorable Robert C. Byrd as President Pro Tempore and Election of the Honorable Strom Thurmond as President Pro Tempore," *Congressional Record*, vol. 147, January 3, 2001, p. 7.

f. Party control in the Senate shifted with the decision in May, 2001, of Senator Jim Jeffords to leave the Republican party and to become an Independent, caucusing with Senate Democrats. On June 6, the Senate agreed to S.Res. 100 electing Senator Byrd President pro tempore once again.

g. Senator Robert C. Byrd died on June 28, 2010. That day, the Senate adopted S.Res. 567, electing Senator Daniel K. Inouye President pro tempore.

h. Senator Daniel K. Inouye died on December 17, 2012. That day, the Senate adopted S.Res. 619, electing Senator Patrick J. Leahy President pro tempore.

The Senate has, on occasion, created special offices connected to the position of President pro tempore. These two positions—detailed below—were created for specific individuals under narrow circumstances and are not currently in use.

Deputy Presidents Pro Tempore

Pursuant to S.Res. 17 (95th Congress), agreed to January 10, 1977, the Senate established (effective January 5, 1977) the post of Deputy President pro tempore of the Senate to be held by "any Member of the Senate who has held the Office of President of the United States or Vice President of the United States." Senator Hubert H. Humphrey was Deputy President pro tempore until his death on January 13, 1978. In the 100th Congress, due to concerns over the health of the President pro tempore, Senator John S. Stennis, the Senate agreed on January 28, 1987, to S.Res. 90, authorizing the Senate to designate a Senator to serve as Deputy President pro tempore during that Congress, in addition to Senators who hold such office under the authority of S.Res. 17 (95th Congress). Accordingly, on the same date the Senate agreed to S.Res. 91 (100th Congress), designating Senator George H. Mitchell Deputy President pro tempore.

Table 9. Deputy Presidents Pro Tempore of the Senate, 1977-2012

Deputy President Pro Tempore	Party	State	Congress	Dates
Hubert H. Humphrey	D	MN	95th	Jan. 5, 1977-Jan. 13, 1978
George J. Mitchell	D	ME	100th	Jan. 28, 1987-Nov. 29, 1988a

a. Senator Mitchell served as Deputy President pro tempore until he was elected majority leader for the 101st Congress on November 29, 1988.

Permanent Acting President Pro Tempore

This post was initially established in 1963 after Senate Majority Leader Michael J. Mansfield became concerned that the stamina of then-President pro tempore, Senator Carl T. Hayden, would be overly taxed by presiding over the prolonged debate on civil rights legislation. In response, the Senate adopted S.Res. 232 and S.Res. 238 (88th Congress) making Senator Lee Metcalf Acting President pro tempore from December 9, 1963, until the meeting of the second session of the 88th Congress. Continuing concerns over the presiding officer's responsibilities led the Senate, on February 7, 1964, to authorize Senator Metcalf "to perform the duties of the Chair as Acting President pro tempore until otherwise ordered by the Senate" via S.Res. 296 (88th Congress). Senator Metcalf held the post throughout his remaining 14 years in the Senate.

Table 10. Permanent Acting President Pro Tempore of the Senate, 1964-2012

Permanent Acting President Pro Tempore	Party	State	Congress	Dates
Lee Metcalf	D	MT	88th-95th	Feb. 7, 1964-Jan. 12, 1978

Party Floor Leader

Each Senate party conference selects its floor leader (also called majority leader or minority leader, as appropriate) in a secret-ballot vote at its organizational meeting prior to the beginning of a new Congress. While these positions developed later than (and arose from) the post of conference chair, they now represent the top post in each party. The majority leader is the lead spokesperson for the party in the chamber and is also responsible for scheduling the legislative activity of the Senate. By precedent established in 1937, the majority leader is afforded priority recognition on the floor. The minority leader leads and speaks for the minority party and is consulted by the majority leader in scheduling Senate floor activity; he also has preferential floor recognition, after the majority leader. The rules of each party conference assign additional responsibilities to each floor leader, as well. In current practice, the floor leader for Senate Democrats also serves as the party's conference chair. (See next section for description of conference chair positions.)

Table 11. Senate Republican Floor Leaders, 1919-2012

Floor Leader	State	Congress	Dates
Henry Cabot Lodge, Sr.[a,b,c]	MA	**66th-68th**	1919-Nov. 9, 1924[d]
Charles Curtis[a,e]	KS	**68th-70th**	Nov. 28, 1924-1929
James E. Watson[a]	IN	**71st-72nd**	1929-1933
Charles L. McNary[a]	OR	73rd-78th	1933-Feb. 25, 1944[f]
Wallace H. White, Jr.	ME	79th **80th**	1945-1949
Kenneth S. Wherry	NE	81st-82nd	1949-Nov. 29, 1951[g]
Styles Bridges	NH	82nd	1952-1953
Robert A. Taft	OH	**83rd**	1953-July 31, 1953[h]
William F. Knowland	CA	83rd 84th-85th	Aug. 4, 1953-1959
Everett Dirksen	IL	86th-91st	1959-Sept. 7, 1969[i]
Hugh Scott	PA	91st-94th	Sept. 24, 1969-1977
Howard H. Baker	TN	95th-96th **97th-98th**	1977-1985
Robert H. Dole	KS	99th 100th-103rd **104th**	1985-June 11, 1996[j]
Trent Lott	MS	**104th-106th** 107th	June 12, 1996 - Dec. 20, 2002[k]
William H. Frist	TN	**108th-109th**	Dec. 23, 200[l]-2007
Mitch McConnell	KY	110th-	2007-

Sources: The principal source for this table is Byrd's *Historical Statistics*, p. 505, with some details provided by Riddick, *Majority and Minority Leaders of the Senate*, pp. 1-11. See the "Source Notes and Bibliography" section at the end of this report for a description and full citation of all sources.

Notes: Bolded entries indicate Congresses in which the floor leader was also majority leader for at least half of the Congress. For example, while the Republicans began the 107th Congress with a controlling majority, party control switched to the Democrats in June of the first session; the 107thCongress is therefore treated as being under Democratic party control in these tables, where applicable.

a.   Indicates a leader who was also conference chair. Prior to 1945, the Republican conference chair and floor leader positions were held by the same individual.

b.   While Byrd's volume provisionally lists Republican Conference Chair Henry Cabot Lodge, Sr, as the first Republican floor leader in practice, some sources treat two previous conference chairs as floor leaders in practice. For example, Riddick includes (in Table III, "Seniority of Majority and Minority Leaders of the Senate," p.11) conference chairs Senator Shelby M. Cullom as majority leader from 1911-1913 and Senator Jacob H. Gallinger as minority leader from 1913 until his death on August 17, 1918.

c.   Elected conference chair in the 65th Congress on August 24, 1918, to replace Senator Gallinger. Senator Lodge was not officially a floor leader; he was simply reelected to the conference chair post in 1919, and the party had not yet employed the designation floor leader. Scholarly opinion is that his role in the 66th to 68th Congresses, for all intents and purposes, was that of the floor leader, however. Byrd's volume provisionally lists him as the first majority leader (Table 4-6, p. 506); Riddick includes him in Table III, p.11. Also see Widenor, "Henry Cabot Lodge: The Astute Parliamentarian," for additional supporting details.

d.   Died in office, November 9, 1924.

e. Senator Charles Curtis was elected conference chair on November 28, 1924, to replace Senator Henry Cabot Lodge, Sr., who died on November 9. On March 5, 1925, the Republican conference also designated him as floor leader, the first Senator to hold the title.

f. Senator Charles L. McNary died on February 25, 1944. There is no reference in congressional sources to the formal selection of a new Republican floor leader during the 78th Congress. In his article summarizing "The Second Session of the Seventy-Eighth Congress (January 10-December 18, 1944)," *American Political Science Review*, vol. 39, April 1945, pp. 317-336, Floyd Riddick makes no mention of McNary's death or the selection of a successor.

g. Died in office, November 29, 1951.

h. Died in office, July 31, 1953.

i. Died in office, September 7, 1969.

j. Resigned from Senate, June 11, 1996.

k. Elected June 12, 1996, to replace Senator Robert H. Dole, and resigned from majority leader post, December 20, 2002.

l. Elected December 23, 2002, to replace Senator Trent Lott.

Table 12. Senate Democratic Floor Leaders and Conference Chairs, 1893-2012

Floor Leader	State	Congress	Dates
Arthur P. Gorman[a,b]	MD	53rd **54th-55th**	1893-1898
N/A[c]		55th-56th	1898-1901
John T. Morgan[b]	AL	57th	1901-1902
James K. Jones[b]	AR	57th	1902-1903
Arthur P. Gorman[d]	MD	58th-59th	1903-June 4, 1906[e]
Joseph C.S. Blackburn[f]	KY	59th	June 9, 1906-1907[g]
Charles A. Culberson	TX	60th	1907-1909
Hernando D. Money	MS	61st	1909-1911
Thomas S. Martin[f]	VA	62nd	1911-1913
John Worth Kern[f]	IN	**63rd-64th**	1913-1917
Thomas S. Martin	VA	**65th** 66th	1917-Nov. 12, 1919[h]
Oscar W. Underwood[f]	AL	66th-67th	Apr. 27, 1920-1923[i]
Joseph T. Robinson	AR	68th-75th **73rd-75th**	1923-July 14, 1937[i]
Alben W. Barkley	KY	75th-79th 80th	July 22, 1937-1949[k]
Scott W. Lucas	IL	**81st**	1949-1951
Ernest W. McFarland	AZ	**82nd**	1951-1953
Lyndon B. Johnson	TX	83rd **84th-86th**	1953-1961
Mike Mansfield	MT	**87th-94th**	1961-1977

Floor Leader	State	Congress	Dates
Robert C. Byrd	WV	95th-96th 97th-99th 100th	1977-1989
George J. Mitchell	ME	**101st-103rd**	1989-1995
Tom Daschle[l]	SD	104th-106th **107th** 108th	1995-2005
Harry Reid	NV	109th **110th-**	2005-

Sources: See the "Source Notes and Bibliography" section at the end of this report for a description and full citation of all sources. The principal source for this table is Byrd's *Historical Statistics,* p. 503. Some additional details are from Riddick's *Majority and Minority Leaders of the Senate,* p. 1-11. Initially the Senate Democratic Caucus, the name was officially changed to the Democratic Conference in 1925.

Notes: Bolded entries indicate Congresses in which the floor leader was also majority leader for at least half of the Congress. For example, while the Republicans began the 107th Congress with a controlling majority, party control switched to the Democrats in June of the first session; the 107th Congress is therefore treated as being under Democratic party control in these tables, where applicable.

a. Byrd's identification of the first Democratic conference chair begins with Senator Gorman in the 58th Congress. Other sources, however, rely on unofficial records to give Gorman that title in the 53rd Congress, with Senators Morgan and Jones identified as such in later Congresses (after a period in which reliable sources do not exist); see, for example, Riddick, *Majority and Minority Leaders of the Senate,* Table I, p. 7.

b. Riddick identifies Senator Gorman as the first Democratic conference chair in 1893, though Byrd does not designate him as such until the 58th Congress. This is also the case with the designations of Senators Morgan in 1901 and Jones in 1902.

c. No reliable records from the caucus exist for this period.

d. Senator Gorman's designation as conference chair in the 58th Congress is the first that can be confirmed from official caucus minutes.

e. Died June 4, 1906.

f. Secondary sources generally identify Senator Kern as the first Democratic floor leader in the modern sense of the term. See, for example, Oleszek, "John Worth Kern," p. 10. Others have made a case for designating Senator Blackburn as the first, since he was referred to as the Democrats' "chosen official leader" in a congratulatory resolution. See Riddick, p. 3. Still others consider Senator Martin an early floor leader; see Oleszek, "John Worth Kern," note 13. Senator Underwood is the first person to be officially called floor leader in minutes of the party conference, so some sources (e.g., Byrd) treat him as the first Democratic floor leader.

g. Elected June 9, 1906.

h. Died November 12, 1919. An initial caucus vote to replace Senator Martin resulted in a tie between Senator Gilbert M. Hitchcock and Senator Underwood. Hitchcock briefly was acting leader until Underwood was elected in April of 1920. See Riddick, p. 9, note 2

i. Elected April 27, 1920.

j. Died July 14, 1937.

k. Elected July 22, 1937.

l. In the 107th Congress, Senator Daschle became majority leader on June 6, 2001, following a change in party control of the Senate from Republican to Democratic.

Conference Chair

Each party has a conference organization consisting of all the elected Senators from that party; it is the main body through which the party contingent at large decides and communicates its legislative priorities. While each party's conference chair posts were the first formal party leadership positions in the Senate, eventually floor leader positions were established as uppermost in each party's leadership hierarchy. Since 1945, Republicans have elected their conference chair separately from other leadership posts, but the elected Democratic floor leader also serves as chair of the Democratic Conference. (See **Table 12** for the list of Democratic floor leaders/conference chairs.)

Table 13. Senate Republican Conference Chairs, 1893-2012

Chair	State	Congress	Dates
John Sherman[a]	OH	53rd **54th**	1893-1897
William B. Allison	IA	**55th-56th**	1897-1901[b]
Eugene Hale	ME	**57th**	1901-1902
Orville Platt	CT	**57th**	1902-1903[c]
Eugene Hale	ME	**58th**	1903-1904
William B. Allison	IA	**58th-59th**	1904-1906
Eugene Hale	ME	**59th**	1906-1907
William B. Allison[d]	IA	**59th**	1907-1908
Nelson W. Aldrich	RI	**60th**	1908-1909
Eugene Hale	ME	**60th-61st**	1909-1910
Shelby M. Cullom	IL	**61st-62nd**	1910-1913
Jacob H. Gallinger	NH	63rd-65th	1913-1918
Henry Cabot Lodge, Sr.[e]	MA	65th **66th-68th**	1918-1924
Charles Curtis[e]	KS	**68th-70th**	1924-1929
James E. Watson[e]	IN	**71st-72nd**	1929-1932
Charles L. McNary[e]	OR	73rd-78th	1933-1944
Arthur H. Vandenberg	MI	79th	1945-1946
Eugene D. Millikin	CO	80th-82nd **83rd** **84th**	1947-1956
Leverett Saltonstall	MA	85th-89th	1957-1966
Margaret Chase Smith	ME	90th-92nd	1967-1972
Norris Cotton	NH	93rd	1973-1974
Carl T. Curtis	NE	94th-95th	1975-1978
Robert Packwood	OR	96th	1979-1980
James A. McClure	ID	**97th-98th**	1981-1984
John Chafee	RI	**99th**	1985-1990

Chair	State	Congress	Dates
		101st	
Thad Cochran	MS	102nd-103rd 104th	1991-1996
Connie Mack	FL	**105th-106th**	1997-2000
Richard J. Santorum	PA	107th 108th-109th	2001-2006
Jon L. Kyl	AZ	110th	2007-Dec. 6, 2007[f]
Lamar Alexander	TN	110th-112th	Dec. 6, 2007[f]-Jan. 26, 2012[g]
John Thune	SD	112th-	Jan. 26, 2012-

Sources: See the "Source Notes and Bibliography" section at the end of this report for a description and full citation of all sources. The principal source for this table is Byrd's *Historical Statistics*, p. 502. Additional detail is from Riddick, *Majority and Minority Leaders of the Senate*, pp. 7-9). Records of the Republican Conference are extant only from 1911. Secondary sources (see Riddick, pp. 7-9) provide information for years prior to 1893. Rothman, in his work, claims that Senator Henry B. Anthony served as Republican caucus chair for an undetermined number of years beginning in 1869 and that Senator George Franklin Edmunds served as chair from 1885 to 1891. See David J. Rothman, *Politics and Power: The United States Senate, 1869-1901*, Cambridge, MA: Harvard University Press, 1966, pp. 6, 28-30.

Notes: Bolded entries indicate Congresses in which the Republican party was in the majority for at least half of the Congress. For example, while the Republicans began the 107th Congress with a controlling majority, party control switched to the Democrats in June of the first session; the 107th Congress is therefore treated as being under Democratic party control in these tables, where applicable. Except for those individuals who also served as floor leader (as designated in next note), sources do not provide specific dates of conference chair service (e.g., when there was a death or resignation and, as a result, a mid-session election was held). Therefore, this table provides only years of service for each conference chair and gives no specific dates for transitions that occurred within a session.

a. Riddick indicates that secondary sources confirm Sherman as the first Republican conference chair (Table I, p.7); Byrd starts his list (Table 4-1, p.502) with Allison's tenure in the 55th Congress, but notes Sherman's previous tenure in a footnote.

b. Byrd lists Senator Allison's tenure in the position as 1897-1901, but Riddick maintains that reliable records do not exist for 1898 to 1901.

c. Using unofficial sources, Riddick (Table I, p. 7) indicates that Senator George H. Hoar was briefly conference chair in 1903. Byrd does not include him.

d. Using unofficial sources, Riddick (Table I, p. 7) indicates Senator Allison was chair; Byrd does not include him.

e. Indicates individuals who were simultaneously identified as the floor leader. See **Table 11** of this report.

f. Senator John L. Kyl was elected party whip on December 6, 2007; Senator Lamar Alexander was elected on that day to serve as conference chair.

g. In September, 2011, Senator Lamar Alexander announced his intention to resign from the post, effective January, 2012. Senator John Thune was elected to the position on December 13, 2011, effective January 26, 2012.

Party Whip

Senate Democrats first selected a party whip in 1913; Republicans followed in 1915. Some accounts of these early selections imply that the individuals were initially appointed, but other contemporary accounts refer to conference elections for the posts. (Republicans first formally codified their conference procedures in 1944, making it clear that the whip post was elected by the conference.) Today, each party conference elects a party whip, who is also known in the

Senate as the assistant majority leader or assistant minority leader, depending on the party. Typically, deputy whips are also appointed to assist the whip operation. The whips communicate leadership priorities to the party rank-and-file (and vice versa), provide leaders an assessment of member support for (or opposition to) pending legislative matters, and mobilize support for leadership-supported measures under consideration. For more information, see CRS Report RS20887, *Senate Leadership: Whip Organization*, by Judy Schneider.

Table 14. Senate Democratic Whips, 1913-2012

Whip	State	Congress	Dates
James Hamilton Lewis[a]	IL	**63rd-65th**	1913-1919
Peter G. Gerry	RI	66th-70th	1919-1929
Morris Sheppard	TX	71st-72nd	1929-1933
James Hamilton Lewis	IL	**73rd-75th**	1933-1939
Sherman Minton	IN	**76th**	1939-1941
J. Lister Hill	AL	**77th-79th**	1941-1947
Scott W. Lucas[b]	IL	80th	1947-1949
Francis J. Myers	PA	**81st**	1949-1951
Lyndon B. Johnson[b]	TX	**82nd**	1951-1953
Earle C. Clement	KY	83rd **84th**	1953-1957
Mike Mansfield[b]	MT	**85th-86th**	1957-1961
Hubert H. Humphrey	MN	**87th-88th**	1961-1965
Russell B. Long	LA	**89th-90th**	1965-1969
Edward M. Kennedy	MA	**91st**	1969-1971
Robert C. Byrd[b]	WV	**92nd-94th**	1971-1977
Alan Cranston	CA	**95th-96th** 97th-99th **100th-101st**	1977-1991
Wendell H. Ford	KY	**102nd-103rd** 104th-105th	1991-1999
Harry Reid[b]	NV	106th, **107th** 108th	1999-2005
Richard Durbin	IL	109th **110th-**	2005-

Sources: See the "Source Notes and Bibliography" section at the end of this report for a description and full citation of all sources. The principal source for this table is Byrd's *Historical Statistics*, p. 509, with additional detail drawn from Oleszek, *Majority and Minority Whips of the Senate*.

Notes: Bolded entries indicate Congresses in which the Democratic whip was also the majority whip for at least half of the Congress. For example, while the Republicans began the 107th Congress with a controlling majority, party control switched to the Democrats in June of the first session; the 107thCongress is therefore treated as being under Democratic party control in these tables, where applicable.

a. Senator James Hamilton Lewis became the first Democratic Party whip in 1913. In the *Congressional Record*, Lewis himself referred to his "appointment," but a press account the next year said he was elected. See Oleszek, *Majority and Minority Whips of the Senate*, p. 4.

b. Indicates individuals who later advanced to floor leader.

Table 15. Senate Republican Whips, 1915-2012

Whip	State	Congress	Dates
James W. Wadsworth, Jr.[a]	NY	64th	1915
Charles Curtis[b]	KS	64th-65th 66th-68th	1915-1924
Wesley L. Jones	WA	68th-70th	1924-1929
Simeon D. Fess	OH	71st-72nd	1929-1933
Felix Hebert	RI	73rd	1933-1935
N/A[c]		74th-77th	1936-1943
Kenneth S. Wherry[b]	NE	78th-79th 80th	1944-1949
Leverett Saltonstall	MA	81st-82nd 83rd 84th	1949-1957
Everett M. Dirksen[b]	IL	85th	1957-1959
Thomas H. Kuchel	CA	86th-90th	1959-1969
Hugh D. Scott[b]	PA	91st	1969
Robert P. Griffin	MI	91st-94th	1969-1977
Ted Stevens	AK	95th-96th 97th-98th	1977-1985
Alan K. Simpson	WY	99th 100th-103rd	1985-1995
Trent Lott[b]	MS	104th	1995-June 12, 1996[d]
Don Nickles	OK	104th-106th 107th	June 12, 1996-2003[e]
Mitch McConnell[b]	KY	108th-109th	2003-2007
Trent Lott	MS	110th	2007-Dec. 6, 2007[f]
Jon L. Kyl	AZ	110th-	Dec. 6, 2007[f]-

Sources: See the "Source Notes and Bibliography" section at the end of this report for a description and full citation of all sources. The principal source for this table is Byrd's *Historical Statistics*, p. 509, with additional details provided by Oleszek, *Majority and Minority Whips of the Senate*.

Notes: Bolded entries indicate Congresses in which the Republican whip was also majority whip for at least half of the Congress. For example, while the Republicans began the 107th Congress with a controlling majority, party control switched to the Democrats in June of the first session; the 107thCongress is treated as being under Democratic party control in these tables, where applicable.

a. Wadsworth was the first Republican whip, but served only one week before Senator Curtis was named his successor. Some sources describe the selections as appointments, but clearly the party eventually elected individuals to the post. The conference rules for such selection were formally codified only in 1944, but the election practice seems to have been occurring prior to this. See Oleszek, *Majority and Minority Whips of the Senate*, p. 5.

b. Indicates individuals who later advanced to floor leader.

c. Between 1936 and 1943, the Republican whip post was filled by informal, irregular appointment by the Republican Leader.

d. Elected majority leader, June 12, 1996.

e. Elected to replace Senator Trent Lott as whip, June 12, 1996.

f. Senator Jon L. Kyl was elected to the position on December 6, 2007, replacing Senator Trent Lott, who resigned from the Senate soon thereafter (on December 18, 2007).

Source Notes and Bibliography

This report relies heavily on primary congressional sources and authoritative documents such as the privately printed *Biographical Directory of the American Congress, 1774 to 1996,* and a similar online adaptation, the *Biographical Directory of the United States Congress, 1774 to the Present.* In addition, over the years, individual Members of Congress, legislative aides, and scholars have gained limited access to party conference journals. Reliable leadership lists have been compiled from these sources. Where these have been published, they have been used as a source in this report. This report also relies on secondary sources developed by scholars. The Congressional Research Service made no attempt to gain access to caucus or conference minutes in collecting data for this report.

Inevitably, conflicting interpretations occur in these data, even among sources generally accepted as reliable. For example, there are disparities on the dates of elections and tenure of Senate Presidents pro tempore between Byrd's history, the 1911 Senate document, and Gamm and Smith's research. The report attempts to footnote these divergences where they occur.

Unless otherwise noted, the following sources were used to compile the tables in this report:

Berdahl, Clarence. "Some Notes on Party Membership in Congress." *American Political Science Review*, vol. 43 (April 1949), pp. 309-332; (June 1949), pp. 492-508; and (August 1949), pp. 721-734.

Biographical Directory of the American Congress, 1774-1996. Washington: CQ Staff Directories Inc., 1997.

Biographical Directory of the United States Congress, 1774 to the Present. Available online at http://bioguide.congress.gov/biosearch/biosearch.asp.

Byrd, Robert C. *The Senate, 1789-1989.* 4 vols., 100th Congress, 1st session. S. Doc. 100-20. Washington: GPO, 1988-1993.

Cannon, Clarence. "Party History." Remarks in the appendix, *Congressional Record*, vol. 89 (January 22, 1941), pp. A383-A384.

Congressional Directory. Washington: GPO, various years.

Congressional Globe. Washington, 1833-1873.

Congressional Quarterly Weekly Report. Washington: Congressional Quarterly, Inc., various dates.

Congressional Record. Washington: GPO, 1873-present.

CRS Report RL30960, *The President Pro Tempore of the Senate: History and Authority of the Office,* by Christopher M. Davis.

Deschler, Lewis. *Deschler-Brown Precedents of the United States House of Representatives.* 16 vols. Washington: GPO, 1977-2000.

Galloway, George B. "Leadership in the House of Representatives." *The Western Political Quarterly,* vol. 12, no. 2, (June 1959), pp. 417-441.

Gamm, Gerald and Steven S. Smith. "Last Among Equals: The Senate's Presiding Officer." In Burdett A. Loomis, ed., *Esteemed Colleagues: Civility and Deliberation in the U.S. Senate,* pp. 105-134. Washington: Brookings Institution Press, 2000.

Martis, Kenneth C. *The Historical Atlas of Political Parties in the United States Congress, 1789-1989.* New York: Macmillan, 1989.

Oleszek, Walter J. *Majority and Minority Whips in the Senate*: History and Development of the Party Whip System in the U.S. Senate. 99th Congress, 1st session. S. Doc. 99-23. Washington: GPO, 1985.

———. "John Worth Kern: Portrait of Floor Leader." In Richard A. Baker and Roger H. Davidson, eds., *First Among Equals: Outstanding Senate Leaders of the Twentieth Century,* pp. 7-37. Washington: CQ Press, 1991.

Ripley, Randall B. *Party Leaders in the House of Representatives.* Washington: Brookings Institution Press, 1967.

———. "The Party Whip Organizations in the United States House of Representatives." *American Political Science Review,* vol. 58 (September 1964), pp. 561-576.

Rothman, David J. *Politics and Power.* Cambridge, MA: Harvard University Press, 1966.

U.S. Congress. *Hinds' and Cannon's Precedents of the House of Representatives of the United States.* 11 vols. Washington: GPO, 1907-1908, 1935-1941.

———. House. *Journal of the House of Representatives of the United States,* 1789-present, various publishers.

———. Senate. *Journal of the Senate of the United States,* 1789-present, various publishers.

———. *Majority and Minority Leaders of the Senate: History and Development of the Offices of the Floor Leaders*. Prepared by Floyd M. Riddick. 99th Congress, 1st session. S. Doc. 99-3. Washington: GPO, 1985.

———. *President of the Senate Pro Tempore*. 62nd Congress, 2nd session. S.Doc. 62-101. Washington: GPO, 1911.

Widenor, William C. "Henry Cabot Lodge: The Astute Parliamentarian," In Richard A. Baker and Roger H. Davidson, eds., *First Among Equals: Outstanding Senate Leaders of the Twentieth Century*, pp. 38-62. Washington: CQ Press, 1991.

Appendix. Political Party Abbreviations

Adams	Adams
Adams-Clay F	Adams-Clay Federalist
Adams-Clay R	Adams-Clay Republican
AJ	Anti-Jackson
Am	American (Know-Nothing)
Anti-Admin	Anti-Administration
C	Conservative
CRR	Crawford Republican
D	Democrat
F	Federalist
FL	Farmer-Labor
FS	Free Soil
I	Independent
ID	Independent Democrat
IR	Independent Republican
J	Jacksonian
JR	Jacksonian Republican
L	Liberty
LR	Liberal Republican
N	Nullifier
N/A	Party Unknown or No Party Affiliation
NR	National Republican
OP	Opposition
PO	Populist
PR	Progressive
Pro-Admin	Pro-Administration
R	Republican
R(DR)[a]	Jeffersonian, Jeffersonian Republican, or Democratic Republican
RA	Readjuster
S	Silver
SR	Silver Republican
U	Unionist
UU	Unconditional Unionist
W	Whig

Source: This table is derived from Byrd, *Historical Statistics*, p. xvi.

a. While the *Biographical Directory of the American Congress, 1774-1996* identifies the party affiliation of certain Representatives in early Congresses as Republicans, the designation "Democratic Republican" is more familiar to readers. This designation, R(DR), should not be taken to refer to the contemporary Republican Party, which did not emerge until the 1850s.

Author Contact Information

Valerie Heitshusen
Analyst on Congress and the Legislative Process
vheitshusen@crs.loc.gov, 7-8635

Acknowledgments

This report was originally written and updated by Paul S. Rundquist and Richard C. Sachs, former Specialists in American National Government at CRS, and Faye M. Bullock, former Technical Information Specialist at CRS. The listed author has updated and expanded this report and is available to respond to inquiries on the subject